PRESENTED TO:

_____

FROM:

_____

DATE:

_____

SIMPLE JOYS

Candace Payne

SIMPLE JOYS

DISCOVERING WONDER IN THE EVERYDAY

ZONDERVAN®

ZONDERVAN

Simple Joys

Copyright © 2018 by Candace Payne

This title is also available as a Zondervan ebook.

Requests for information should be addressed to:

Zondervan, *3900 Sparks Dr. SE, Grand Rapids, Michigan 49546*

Library of Congress Cataloging-in-Publication Data
ISBN 978–0–310089858 (HC)
ISBN 978–0–310090731 (eBook)

Author is represented by The Christopher Ferebee Agency, www.christopherferebee.com.

Art direction: Micah Kandros
Interior design: Mallory Collins

Printed in China

18 19 20 21 22   DSC   10 9 8 7 6 5 4 3 2 1

For Larry, Barbara, Mark, Tami, and David.
There has never been anything like
the joy I have shared with you.
I love you more than I could ever write, sing, or say.

"I have told you this so that my joy may be in you and that your joy may be complete."

—John 15:11

CONTENTS

THERE'S JOY IN THEM HILLS!

I feel as though I should start this entire journey toward joy with a confession. I absolutely *love* reality television. Don't judge me. I know. I feel it through the pages. I get how amazing awful it is. Yet I cannot stop watching. And it's not as if I just watch one particular category or genre of reality TV. No, if it's real-ish life, I'm there. From teenage moms to people living in the bush in Alaska, I will watch them all. One show in particular (that I have successfully snared my husband's attention with as well) is one where they follow the journey of a few different rag-tag companies mining for gold. I don't know how or why this show became one of our favorites. Maybe it's the burly voice-over, the nifty graphic blueprint illustrations that explain "what-on-earth" terms exclusive to the mining world, or the fact that you never know if they're going to be successful finding gold or not. I am drawn to the lives of the people mining. I'm intrigued: Why would they risk so much time from their families and invest so much money on equipment on something that may or may not *pan out*? (Y'all. I didn't even try to put that pun there. It just happened.) Seriously, though. Why waste so much effort and sacrifice so much for something like that? I've seen grown men jump up and down on this show over the tiniest speck of gold.

The idea of gold mining isn't a new thing. It's rather old in our world. History has seen many a gold rush and many a person with "gold fever." Can you even imagine the feeling of unearthing dirt and rock that look like nothing special, only to find one of the most valuable elements known to humanity hiding inside? It is a treasure hunt of epic proportions. And when I say *treasure*, that's an understatement. There is nothing quite like gold here on earth.

Likewise, I have come to discover there is nothing quite like joy here on earth. And maybe the attraction I have to the television screen as I watch the struggles and successes in gold mining has something to do with the way they mirror my own struggles and successes in finding joy. It has become a beautiful metaphor for uncovering the places we often overlook to find joy in our lives.

As you read through this book, I want you to become a prospector for joy. My hope for you is that you begin digging in unearthed places to discover pure joy—just as eagerly as you would dig for pure gold. Go ahead. Lift your eyes and hopes up through each chapter—because there's *joy* in them hills!

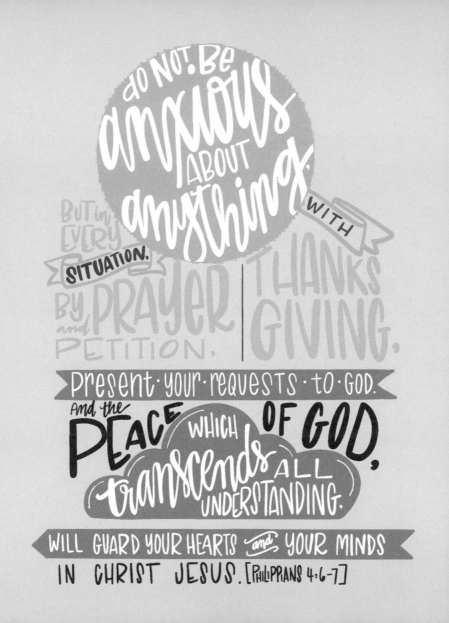

do not be anxious about anything. but in every situation, by prayer and petition, with thanksgiving, present your requests to god. and the peace of god, which transcends all understanding, will guard your hearts and your minds in christ jesus. [Philippians 4:6-7]

THE YEAR I SPENT WITH MY HEAD IN THE CLOUDS

I was performing a skit I wrote for a summer camp crowd of nearly three hundred students, ages twelve to eighteen, on a stage in a large room that resembled a log cabin nestled in the mountains of Colorado. Suddenly someone handed me an urgent message on a Post-it note asking me to call my sister. It simply read:

Call home.

9–1–1.

Now, this was a few years before cell phones were in the hands of everyone. I know, I know. How did this world function without cell phones? In fact, we had these things called "pay phones." And yes, true to their descriptive title, you had to pay to use them. With actual coins. Yeah. Insane.

Nevertheless, I ran down rocky steps and through tall pine trees until I saw a light shining from the one giant pole that also held the electrical wires that supplied the dorms and camp cafeteria with modern comforts and electricity. At its base was a pay phone. I picked up the receiver and prayed that I could withstand whatever news would come my way. Just weeks earlier, I had buried my sweet Grandpa Sharp (the first grandparent I had lost). I couldn't bear much more news of death in my family, but I was trying to prepare my heart for what might come. I dialed and waited for what seemed like a year with each ring. My sister finally answered, and I rushed to cut her off with, "I'm here. Got your message. What's up?"

My sister hesitated to start her sentence but was direct once she did: "Okay. Well, I just saw on the news that your choir was in a plane crash. It's your friends. David. Bonnie. Allison. You need to find a TV to see what's going on and then try to come home."

June 1, 1999, was the date.

I had just finished my sophomore year of college and was in an elect choir called the Ouachita Singers. Most of this choir had gone on an overseas trip that summer to perform in Europe at different churches and venues. It was an elective trip, since you would have to raise funds to go and pay your own way. When given the option, I didn't want to go, but instead chose to work at the summer camp where I had worked the year before. A handful of others didn't go either, but most did. I was in shock. I had no clue who had survived, if any, of my core group of friends. I was gripped with fear and grief that I had lost them all. It wasn't until about an hour later that I got more facts about what had happened.

American Airlines, flight 1420. It was the last leg of the trip home from their choir concert adventures, and the plane crashed as it flew from Dallas-Fort Worth to Little Rock, Arkansas. Eleven of the 145 people aboard, the captain and ten passengers, were killed in the crash. One of those passengers was a twenty-one-year-old friend who lost his life when he refused to stop entering the flames to drag people to safety after the plane had crashed. He was a hero and a quiet young man who spent his life, quite literally, serving others. And our beloved choir director and his strong and sassy wife (who was also our accompanist and my personal voice teacher)

I GET A FEELING OF WONDER EVERY TIME I LOOK OUT A WINDOW TO SEE THAT MY HEAD IS LITERALLY IN THE CLOUDS.

would have to bury one of their young daughters just days later due to injuries sustained during the crash.

I came home. I met with my friends who had survived. I hugged necks. I cried. I stayed quiet and let them talk. And we all tried to pick up the pieces of our lives the following semester as classes resumed.

Because of this event in my life at the age of twenty, I do not love to fly. I have seen the effects, firsthand, that come with the grief, loss, and devastation a crash leaves behind.

Call me sensitive, if you like, but I wouldn't even watch a movie if I knew it had a plane crash scene in it. I was in avoidance mode. I didn't want to remember that year following the crash and the effects it had on my friends, our community, and our joy.

Now fast-forward nearly twenty years. It was May 19, 2016, when I posted the "Chewbacca Mom" video that went viral. If you're reading this, you may already have seen it and know about the video. But for those who don't know, it's a four-minute video with three minutes of pure laughter and joy I experienced while wearing a toy mask that made funny sounds as I opened and closed my mouth. Sounds fun, right? Well, it was. I laughed and laughed like I hadn't laughed in years. And as the world began to share that video, that laugh became viral overnight and infected nearly a hundred million viewers within days. I started getting invitations to appear on different television shows. Now, these shows were not a hop, skip, and jump away from my home. Nope. I had to fly in an airplane to get there. By June 1 (the anniversary date of Flight 1420's fatal crash), I had flown six times since I posted the video less than two weeks previously. This was more than I had flown in the preceding eighteen years. Though I tried to enjoy every moment this fun and funny little viral video granted me, I was also gripped with fear and insecurity during every takeoff and landing.

I kept on flying to media events and speaking engagements the following year. I did it so much, I learned how to navigate through security and not be "that lady" who holds up the line because she doesn't know all the rules. You know. The one who brings a giant bottle of aerosol hairspray and a large coffee through the line while wearing lace-up boots that take about ten minutes each to take off. These days I have it down. I wear easy-off shoes to the airport and never wear a belt. I always have a ziplock baggie full of appropriately ounced liquid toiletries. I don't mean to brag, but I've got this. I even came up with my own go-to routines to calm and course-correct my nerves during takeoff and landing. When I fly, I am never without the thought of that season from the crash, but I have learned a way not only to cope but to do fairly well as a frequent flier.

One thing I always love to do while flying is look outside the plane window and see the clouds. On bright, sunny days I find myself in awe of where I am, if only for a few minutes. I mean, that is an underrated simple joy I see passengers ignore every

EVEN ·IN THE· MOST FEARFUL circumstance, yes, even IN THE valley OF THE SHADOW OF DEATH, 〈it is〉 POSSIBLE TO FEEL safe.

flight. Some get it, though. They are the ones you see lift the shade at the risk of waking their fellow row rider, push up their seat, lean forward, and stare. I get a feeling of wonder every time I look out a window to see that my head is literally in the clouds. All the fear I feel in getting up there and then coming back down to earth is washed away when I peer at the vast expanse of sky, clouds, and sunshine. It's a hidden place where I find a secret habitat not many get to see. Within the year following that viral video, I flew more than forty thousand miles. That has helped me retrain my mind to know that crashes aren't the norm. I have slowly and surely found enjoyment in traveling in the clouds. I have even, a few times, found takeoff and landing to be an afterthought. My hands no longer clutch the armrest but, instead, are folded in my lap or engaged in expression as I talk with a new friend I've made in the seat next to mine. It has taken a year in the clouds to find the peace that has afforded me the simple joys of all the things flying can be: fun, exhilarating, and wonder-full. Now, if you'd told me a year ago that I would ever describe flying in those terms, I would have looked at you as if you were crazy. But one flight with my children, in particular, gave me new cause to see it just like that.

———

It was a last-minute request to come and speak for a friend at her church. I would need to fly myself (and my kiddos with me) from Fort Smith, Arkansas, to Sacramento, California, the following morning. I didn't have time to pre-pare my thoughts for flying. Preparation had become a huge advantage in calming my nerves . . . but this time I couldn't. Nevertheless, I was with my children, and my "momma bear" instincts overtook anything

WHEN YOU FEEL SAFE, YOU ALLOW SPACE FOR JOY.

else I would feel. We made it in plenty of time to the airport with moments to spare for last-minute restroom breaks and a coffee run for myself. My son was seven years old; my daughter was eight. It was right in the middle of their summer break, and we were all excited about the spontaneous weekend adventure awaiting us in Cali. We settled into our seats and pulled out our handheld devices to entertain and distract us. The flight took off smoothly, and we were served snacks and drinks without a hiccup in the air. But during the last twenty minutes of the flight, we began to experience mild turbulence that would quickly turn into severe turbulence. And, y'all, I don't say that lightly. This was crazy. I had felt turbulence that was choppy, but this was more than that. We began to jolt furiously. It felt as though we were in the hands of an irresponsible, giant toddler in the sky playing with a toy airplane being swooshed and wooshed from side to side. I was not the only one who became genuinely concerned for our safety. A woman behind me began to yell in fear with grunts of "*ooooh*" and "*please, God, no*" mixed in. At times the crowd let out a unified gasp of fear. Except this was no thrill ride at an amusement park; our lives depended on a metal tube in the air fighting desperately to defy gravity. Everyone knew it. Well, everyone except my seven-year-old son.

Duncan also began to make a ruckus as we flip-flopped in the air. But it was a ruckus of pure joy! I looked over to see him with his hands raised high in the air, laughing and screaming in exhilaration. My initial thought was, *What is wrong with him?! Doesn't he know we are all going to die?!* Then, after what seemed like an eternity the plane leveled out, and we all recovered our throats from the pit of our stomachs. But not my Duncan. Nope. He was yelling to me (as though I weren't sitting directly next to him), "Mom! That was *awesome*! Can we do it again? Please?" I looked at his innocent face and the naivety hidden behind his sweet question and learned something about simple joys in that moment.

Duncan didn't just see the danger as an adventure (and that alone is a lesson worth more than gold). No, my son taught me that joy was more accessible when we feel safe.

Being safe and feeling safe are often not synonymous with each other.

Yet . . .

All Duncan knew was that his momma was with him and would keep him safe no matter what. I find this beautiful truth also has a place in my faith. As a person who not only

YOU CAN LAUGH AND LET GO WITH HANDS RAISED HIGH WHEN LIFE GETS TURBULENT INSTEAD OF CLUTCHING THE ARMRESTS OF INSECURITIES AND FEAR.

claims to believe in God but places her trust in God, I have experienced joy so many times solely because I believe I am safe in His hands.

I don't know what your gauge for safety and security is. But I do know that when you feel safe, you allow space for joy. You find adventure no matter the outside danger. You can laugh and let go with hands raised high when life gets turbulent instead of clutching the armrests of insecurities and fear. And that is a simple joy I long to know each and every day—especially when I am in the thick of fear.

Is there anything in your life right now that gives you a feeling of wonder? If not, is there an adventure that's been on your heart you'd like to pursue that could lead you to wonder?

_____

_____

_____

_____

_____

_____

_____

_____

_____

_____

_____

_____

_____

_____

_____

_____

_____

_____

_____

_____

_____

_____

_____

_____

TRASH-BAG CHOIR DRESSES
AND THE COLLEGE CRUSH

*S*wish, *swish, swoosh, swoosh.*

You could hear the sound a mile away from our black concert choir dresses as we lined the hallway, preparing to perform in one of the most beautiful, ornate, and historic churches in the South. We always wore uniform dresses and tuxedos when we performed as a group. They were a mandatory purchase if you were selected for this elite college choir. But I never would have worn this dress if it weren't required, and here's why: In all honesty, it looked and sounded like a trash bag that someone cut a hole in the top of for the head and cinched up at the waist. It was taffeta. Its sleeves were so giant and puffy that they would make the '80s (yes, the entire decade of the 1980s) jealous. There was no proper undergarment choice to make it look more slimming or more desirable since it hugged every single body frame the same way. It always made loud sounds as you moved in it. Heck, mine would even make a small rustle as I'd breathe in and out.

When I got this dress, it was custom-tailored to fit me perfectly. But my college obsession with Jack in the Box tacos would soon change that. I'd always get a craving an hour or so before each concert. What's worse, I eventually developed a silly superstition that I had to eat two tacos before every performance to be my best. Bloating and meat sweats were par for the course back in the day. (*Wow. Do you ever hear yourself say something that you* should *be embarrassed and ashamed about as it comes out of your mouth, yet instead you embrace the truth about it and just roll with it? Yeah. Me neither. Moving on.*) Beyond the normal ruckus from the dresses, there was a certain echo to their every swing and bustle as we lined up that day.

The church we were standing in was built in the early 1900s and had exquisite stained-glass artwork. Handcrafted wooden pews lined the small sanctuary, and the floor featured the original, narrow planks of hardwood. The acoustics that

IF IT'S POSSIBLE TO SAY THAT YOU FEEL "BOSS" AND LIKE A "BAD MAMMA JAMMA" ABOUT BEING A CHOIR KID, THIS WAS THE MOMENT YOU'D OWN THAT FEELING.

resonated and reverberated around the wide-open space from floor to ceiling were a choir kid's dream. Just not so conducive to getting around in the hefty, autumn-leaf-gathering trash-bag dresses we wore.

I was standing in line in my usual spot—two people away from *him*. It's not necessary to name him—let's just say it's the "him" we've all had at some point in our quest to find someone to date and marry. He was funny, cute (enough), witty, talented, and kindhearted. We'd laugh at the most juvenile things about movies and ourselves. Others would join in on the fun we seemed to create whenever we were together. He wrote me notes to encourage me when I felt lost in the sea of new people and challenges I faced as a young college adult four hours away from home. He made sure I was safely in my dorm room when we'd leave a group of people and return to campus together. Yeah. *Him*. Now I can look back and shake my head at how dramatically I pined after him. You see, he didn't end up being the one or *the* him I now love and share all my life with. But to a nineteen-year-old kid with dreams of loving someone and being loved in full, he was all I could think about night and day. Maybe you've been there as well . . . when you've loved someone without merit or reason or romantic connection, but just for the hope that he'd love you the way you never even loved yourself. That was me. And there I was . . . taffeta dress, meat sweats, and two spots away from *him*.

Usually I would stand next to the altos, an appropriate thing to do for a choir—stay in your section. But occasionally the choir director does you a huge honor by trusting you to stand in a formation where you are mixed with other singing parts surrounding you. It means you are good enough to sing your part correctly without having to listen and follow the person next to you. Listen, if it's possible to say that you feel "boss" and like a "bad mamma jamma" about being a choir kid, this was the moment you'd own that feeling. So I was in rare form that day. I was full of tacos, with intensified confidence in my "madd alto skillz," and yet I was a ginormous ball of nervous energy to be near him as well. It was the perfect storm for what would come next.

We swished and swooshed as elegantly as we could to the stage and took our places on the risers. We had several songs to sing that day as honored guests. And since we would be there a while, the church provided some chairs to sit on when we were done singing our special music. Now, these weren't your everyday chairs. This day we were graced with the chairs borrowed from the preschool room adjacent to the church sanctuary we were singing in. You know—the hard, plastic ones that are only about two feet tall. However small they were, I was grateful to have them. I despised standing in that dress for longer than necessary.

The choir director's magical wand lifted into the air and took the "ready position," as if he were about to cast a spell on us Harry Potter style. The most exhilarating moment about being in a unified choir is that steady pause with our gazes affixed to the director's wand. It's a moment of perfect silence. It is the nearest I've ever felt to having "Spidey senses" and superpowers in slow motion as depicted in my favorite superhero movies. It meant we were about to experience the magic of many voices, full-bodied, with variations and tones so dissimilar, raised in perfect unity without any other instrument accompanying them. And this elite group did it well. We all loved music and the art of what we were a part of . . . something much bigger than ourselves. We knew it. We felt it. And if for just a few minutes, our spirits soared within the echoes that would dance, playfully jump, and reverberate in the wooden rafters of that vast church ceiling. In a moment like that I felt nearer to the throne room of heaven than any other.

As we finished our last song and ended this sacred, holy moment, applause erupted. We were trained, though, not to respond to any praise or applause whatsoever. We were like hungry lions stalking the prey of our director's wand, and we wouldn't move until we had the go-ahead to breathe and rest our shoulders. We were steady and unshakable. Finally, the director gave the signal to stand at ease, and we began to take our seats. With a sense of deep satisfaction and a euphoric feeling of accomplishment, I looked to my right just as *he* began to look to his left. We locked eyes. Y'all. Was this moment *the* moment when he'd finally realize I was everything he was dreaming about too? (*Please, please, please . . . let it be!*)

With eyes still locked on target, I refused to be the first

WE ALL HAVE A CHOICE IN HOW WE RESPOND WHEN EXPECTATIONS DON'T MEET REALITY. WE CAN EITHER FLEE IN FEAR OR STAND TALL AND LAUGH!

to look away. I noticed he was gently lowering himself toward the seat behind him. As he moved, I took his cue and also began to crouch backward. In slow motion, as we moved together toward our low-to-the-ground-hard-plastic school chairs, his eyes shifted toward the floor behind me. His expression swiftly turned from a small smile to a concerned frown. I was not only missing the corner of this tiny chair, but was also about to miss the entire riser that I had been standing so confidently on just seconds before. As I fell, my trash-bag dress blew up like a wind had taken hold of it in a supermarket parking lot. Before I knew what was happening, I was completely upside down, dress over my head, and face flushed the brightest red. I collected myself, pushed my dress down to its rightful position, rocked back and forth trying to gain momentum to get upright, and finally stood up with all eyes on me. Time was frozen. I was frozen. Faces of friends, my choir director, and hundreds of strangers looked frozen with concern as well. And I had a choice to make. Would I rush off stage and hide from embarrassment? Or would I laugh at what had just happened and own the moment?

I believe we have moments like these every day. No, they may not look quite like *this* moment. But they are moments when we feel like a failure—exposed beyond the reach of what we were willing to share. They are moments we find ourselves falling hard right after performing at some of our mountainous bests. We might feel embarrassed because of who saw us fall. Yet I have found these aren't just moments, but opportunities.

We all have a choice in how we respond when expectations don't meet reality. We can either flee in fear or stand tall and laugh!

As the frozen moment of all eyes on me began to thaw, I was embarrassed. I also knew that this was hilarious. When I stood to my feet and shoved the dress back down, I did what I know best to do: I let out a boisterous laugh. Suddenly it was as if everyone took

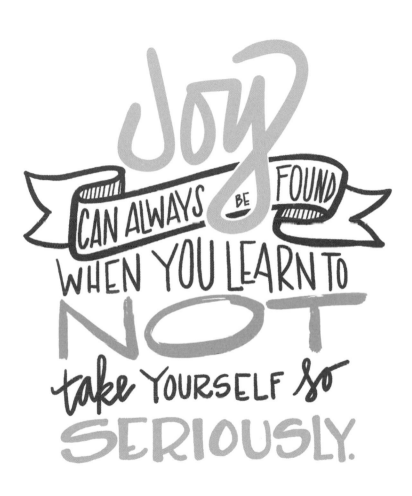

Joy can always be found when you learn to NOT take yourself so SERIOUSLY.

a cue in how to respond and began to laugh *with* me. I wasn't faking this moment and hiding behind a laugh. No, not one bit. I thought of what it must have looked like from the audience's perspective, and a smile made its way across my face and uncontrollable laughter followed. I wondered what *he* must have been thinking of me . . . and as I looked up at him, he was standing with a hand out to make sure I wasn't hurt. And I realized something monumental in that moment about simple joys: *joy can always be found when you learn to not take yourself so seriously.*

Oh, the joy we often miss out on when we flee in fear when, instead, we should stand in confidence and laugh out loud.

THERE'S A DEEP CONFIDENCE THAT CONFESSES, "THIS IS NOT THE END OF MY STORY, AND IT WON'T BE THE WORST OF IT EITHER!"

Proverbs 31 talks about how a truly noble and honorable woman should behave and act and live. (Y'all know I could use all the lessons I can get.) One of my favorite verses says it like this:

She always faces tomorrow with a smile. (v. 25 THE MESSAGE)

Another version puts it this way:

She can laugh at the days to come.

No matter what comes—the fear of days unknown or uncertainty with health and finances—there's power in standing up to whatever you're facing with a smile and a laugh. There's a deep confidence that confesses, "This is not the end of my story, and it won't be the worst of it either!"

That moment with my college crush and the entire audience seeing me with my dress over my head wasn't the end of my days. Sure, it was embarrassing. Yes, it kinda damaged the hope of ever crossing the friend zone with *him*. But something in me knew it was better to laugh and know this was just a moment. And wouldn't you know it, about twenty years later, I still laugh when I retell this story. It was an opportunity to be brave, confident, and humbled that I wasn't about to miss.

Where in your life have you been refusing to get up off the ground and break the atmosphere with a laugh? If a situation comes to mind immediately, know this: it's never too late to shift your response. I know firsthand that life can bring you down without warning. I know full well that it can feel overwhelming. I know the temptation to run away in shame instead of standing tall and owning your mistakes (and, even worse, owning your arrogance). The most beautiful thing about joy in moments like these is how it reflects a humble heart.

So, friend, if you've been taking yourself a bit

too seriously of late, or if you feel overexposed and embarrassed by choices you've made intentionally or unintentionally, take some time to muster a smile and know that simple joys thrive in your humility.

What makes you feel "boss" and like a "bad mamma jamma"?

_____

_____

_____

_____

_____

_____

_____

_____

_____

_____

_____

SIMPLE JOYS

"for we LIVE BY faith, [BY] NOT sight."

2 CORINTHIANS 5:7

THE WATERBED WHERE
I SAID, "AMEN"

My dad, Larry, is an entrepreneur at heart. He has owned a few businesses in his day. From lawn care to pressure washing, my dad knows what it means to make an honest living with the skills he has. It's not that he could never work under someone else's authority. Rather, he's had incredible ideas and thought up systems for doing things in a way that is often more efficient than what's already in place.

One of my favorite entrepreneurial adventures he pursued was owning a waterbed store. Now, I feel I need to stop some of you right here and now and explain what a waterbed is. Did you have one back in the day? Because they were amazing. You know the feeling of sleeping on a floatie in the pool on a warm summer day and being taken away by the lazy drift of tiny waves? Yeah. Owning a waterbed was a lot like that—and even better because you achieved that same feeling while being in the air-conditioning under snugly comforters. Some waterbeds could even heat up with the push of a button. Just magical. Why we did away with that trend, I will never understand. (Might be due to the fact that they'd spring a leak every now and then, but is that really worth complaining about? I kid. There are good safety-related reasons that trend died down, I am sure.) Oh, but Larry's Waterbed Store was the place to be back then! And, naturally, we had a waterbed in every bedroom at one point. So it's no wonder that one of my favorite memories is sitting between my mom and dad on a waterbed while we said our nighttime prayers. But on one particular night, a simple waterbed prayer led to extravagant joy.

We had just gotten back from a Southern gospel singin' service. Now, if you're from the Bible Belt, you may be familiar with this phrase. If you're not, no need to fret. I can fill you in quickly. You see, on a Saturday night, once a month, people in the church who wanted to sing, but didn't get to, would get together and bring a song or a hymn. That probably sounds a bit tacky, the way I described it just now, but I am being as honest as I can from the viewpoint of a six-year-old. Some of these folks may have been talented, but more often than not, there was good reason they weren't allowed to sing on a Sunday

A SIMPLE WATERBED PRAYER LED TO EXTRAVAGANT JOY.

morning when the service was packed full of both regular attendees and visitors. I remember another gospel singin' service when a lady who always asked to sing a solo on Sundays had her day in the spotlight. You usually played an instrument to accompany yourself or brought an accompaniment track to sing along with. This lady did neither. Instead, she got up on stage and began to discourse about how she was going to sing her own "jazzy rendition" of "His Eye Is on the Sparrow" without any musical background. No accompaniment whatsoever. Now, this was my cue to really perk up and pay attention. When she started singing, it took everything I had not to get the giggles. I couldn't help it. Every time she sang the lyrics "I sing because," she put a weird emphasis on a break that is not naturally in the word *because* that sounded like a chicken clucking. You best believe I *lived* for the gospel singin' nights. They were wonderful in many ways. And another night in particular was no exception.

I was six years old, so I wasn't paying too much attention to what was happening on the stage at the gospel singin' service. I was lost in the wide-ruled notebook my mom would let me draw pictures in every time we'd go to church. (I look back now and know that this is why I still love to draw, sketch, and illustrate to this day.) What I didn't realize at the time was how this helped me develop a way of focusing to better retain information while simultaneously drawing and listening. It changed the way I learn and focus. And I *love* that.

Somewhere between drawing a picture of Rainbow Brite, Inspector Gadget, or Garfield, I was captivated by a man speaking on stage at the gospel singin' service. I don't remember the exact words he said, but I know he was describing Jesus. He was describing how much he loved Jesus and why he gave his whole life to follow Jesus because of what Jesus had done for him. It was, for lack of a better description, the first time I recall paying attention to someone while

SIMPLE faith FUELS extravagant joy.

he was sharing the gospel. *Gospel*, by the way, is just a fancy word for good news. And I was curious if the news about a Man willing to give His life on a cross, be beaten beyond recognition, and die for humanity was really "good news" or not.

Well, this man went on to share that the good news was not just in Jesus' dying but in His miraculous rising from the dead so all of us could go to heaven if we just believed. Even now I know some of you reading this may have deep emotions that stir with this retelling. You may feel deep connections of agreement and faith. Others may

WHEN YOU CHOOSE TO BELIEVE SOMETHING SO SEEMINGLY IMPOSSIBLE, YOU HAVE TO TELL OF THE WONDER AND FAITH FOUND IN IT AND HOW IT HAS SHAPED YOU.

experience bitterness because you feel it is a bunch of mythical bedtime storytelling. I want to let you know that I don't aim to convince you of how you should feel or what you should believe as you read my story. But when you choose to believe something so seemingly impossible, you have to tell of the wonder and faith found in it and how it has shaped you.

So that night when we got home, I requested some alone time to ask my mom and dad some serious questions before we went to bed. I climbed on top of their waterbed covered in a patchwork, multicolor, velvet quilt. *People. It was the 1980s, and this thing was uh-mazing!* I told my parents that I believed what the man had said on stage that night and I wanted to give my life to Jesus. And, to be honest, as a six-year-old, I was more concerned with escaping the idea of hell than embracing the hope of heaven. So my parents asked me if I wanted to ask Jesus to live in my heart and, if so, if I would pray a prayer that they'd ask me to repeat as they prayed it aloud. I told them

I wanted that more than anything else in the whole world. We held hands in a circle, and my mom led me in a prayer asking Jesus to come into my heart and promising to follow Him all my life. When we said, "Amen," I thought for sure I'd open my eyes and have some newly developed superhero powers. But I didn't. I did, however, feel a warmth in my heart that flooded me from head to toe. And I just knew, even at the age of six years old, my life would never be the same after that night.

I had taken the first step into an unknown journey toward joy through faith. For the first time I knew firsthand what I would begin to hope was Truth. And soon that hope turned into knowing, and the knowing into faith.

And nearly thirty-five

I HAD TAKEN THE FIRST STEP INTO AN UNKNOWN JOURNEY TOWARD JOY THROUGH FAITH.

years later, I can confidently say that the journey has had its ups and downs, its doubts and decisions. Yet it has always led to a hope that floods my mind and heart with great joy. I don't know where you find faith and what you do to grow it daily. But I do know that simple faith can be the fuel for extravagant joy.

Have you taken your first step toward true joy? If so, recall the circumstances of that experience in your life and how it has shaped you. If not, what's holding you back from beginning your own journey of faith?

_____

_____

_____

_____

_____

_____

_____

_____

_____

_____

_____

_____

_____

_____

_____

_____

_____

_____

_____

_____

_____

_____

_____

_____

_____

MANY, LORD *my* GOD, ARE THE WONDERS YOU HAVE DONE. THE THINGS YOU PLANNED FOR US NONE CAN COMPARE WITH YOU; WERE I TO SPEAK AND TELL OF *your* DEEDS, THERE WOULD BE TOO MANY to DECLARE.

PSALM 40:5

THE HOUSE ON THE HILL, THE COFFEE THAT WOULD SPILL, AND THE STORIES SHARED AROUND THE TABLE

I loved having a big family growing up. A family with four children always means a party of six. And a party of six means that you have to definitively say good-bye to any transportation with only five seats. And boy, have we had some fun cars in the past. Back in the day we didn't have all the swanky Bluetooth-audio-connected, rear-camera-in-the-dash, video-screens-in-headrests luxuries that we have today. (Although I felt we were ballin' that one time we had an Econovan with window shades and a VCR player and flip-down screen from the head-liner. Never mind the headliner cloth was drooping to where you couldn't see the screen when it flipped down . . . straight ballin' nonetheless.) We had some doozies with bench seats that the four of us would share. Now, before you get up in arms about safety, you have to realize, times were different. We didn't know what we know now. I am pretty sure my brother, David, and I shared one long lap belt for a solid two years in the back of a Lincoln Town Car. And, looking back, that was a miracle and test of the integrity of the seatbelt itself, with all the adolescent girth it had to secure. It was a way different time for transportation altogether.

Not only did we have many different cars growing up, but we had different houses as well. Some were more memorable than others. In my book *Laugh It Up*, I describe the nomadic life in more detail, but for now, just know this: we moved *a lot*. One house in particular was a favorite of mine for a short-lived season. It was a house on a hill. I always wanted a house on a hill. Because it stood head and shoulders above the others, you could see the porch light from nearly three blocks away. It called to me and invited me with warmth and cheeriness in a very transient season. Not only was the position of this house beautiful, but it had one thing that I want in a home still to this day: a half-circle driveway. Now, I don't know how you visualized things as you read, but did you catch that? It had a half-circle driveway on a very tall and steep hill. This means we always had to park our bulky car on a sideways slant when we'd get home. If you opened that door slanted toward the street, you'd practically need a forklift to get it closed again.

The hill was that steep. I loved that house. In wintertime it was so much fun to grab a cardboard box and slide down that snowy hill to the bottom. And in the spring I cannot tell you how many times I would lay flat and roll down the hill trying to beat my personal record of twelve tumbles. I never could. But hey—#personalbest. Now, did my parents and siblings love that house as much as I did? Doubtful. As a matter of fact, I think my dad cussed the house on the hill one Sunday in particular.

My dad never, and when I say never . . . I mean *never* . . . puts a lid on any cup he is drinking from. The first thing he does when he gets a soda from a drive-through window is savagely rip off the plastic lid and throw the straw over his shoulder so that he can get his lips on the side of the cup to inhale (quite loudly) ice cubes. Then comes the chomping. Y'all. You want to know how I know my mother genuinely loves my dad after *fifty* years of marriage? It's the fact that she knew early on the sounds her husband would

HE HAD A BIG, BLACK BIBLE WITH GOLD-FOILED EDGES TUCKED IN ONE HAND LIKE A PRO FOOTBALL PLAYER HEADING DOWN TOWARD THE END ZONE, AND A COFFEE CUP (WITH NO LID AND FILLED TO THE BRIM) IN THE OTHER.

make while he ate and drank . . . and she stayed. She is a much stronger woman than I.

And just because this feels a bit therapeutic to share this, might I add to the chomping the sound he makes when he rummages through a popcorn bucket at the movie theater? Like, what are you hoping to find down there, Larry? Envision being a teenager with your parents in a small-town movie theater and having them sit a row behind you as you "double date." All I could hear was the rustling of my dad's calloused, giant hand sifting through the bucket behind us accompanied by the smacking. Who wants to hold hands or think about stealing a kiss crouched down in the seats when all you hear behind you is the sound of two dogs fighting over a piece of meat? What? Too specific? Well, it felt really good to get that out. I still, to this day, do not know someone who eats or drinks as loudly or voraciously as my father.

My dad always made me nervous with his disdain for drink lids. I don't stress out too easily. I may have broad and fully emotional responses, but internally nothing really makes me freak out. Nothing except when my dad would come to the car on a Sunday morning with his coffee in hand. The man owned more than five thermoses. They had lids. But, in true to Larry fashion, even when he'd use a thermos, he'd use the lid as another cup. Inevitably we'd hear the occasional cuss word as drips of piping-hot coffee would splash onto his stomach or crotch. I could never decide if that was accidental holiness or not. I just knew whatever he was saying to that cup of uncovered coffee was serious business.

One Sunday when the streets were covered with just enough ice to make you careful where you'd step, but not enough to warrant staying off the roads, my dad truly tested his no-lid, coffee-carrying skills like never before. My mom grabbed the car keys and sounded the alarm. We had roughly five minutes to be BIS (behind-in-seat) before we left for church that morning. I remember her turning over the car and hearing the sputter of the cold engine getting courage to growl against the winter frost several times before it huffed and puffed and eventually purred. The five of us sat buckled and dressed in our Sunday best as we tried desperately to feel warmth come from the vents of that car. Finally, we saw Dad emerge onto the front porch, turning around to lock the front door before heading toward the family car to take his driver's seat. And wouldn't you know it? He had a big, black Bible with gold-foiled edges tucked in one hand like a pro football player heading down toward the end zone and a coffee cup (with no lid and filled to the brim) in the other.

Daddy usually wore cowboy boots. This Sunday was no exception. He had on a neatly starched and pressed business suit, white shirt, and coordinating tie elegantly done in a Windsor knot. He was a dapper dresser, having grown up in a generation that took pride in wearing a suit and tie for regular occasions. As a matter of fact, every Saturday evening after dinner he'd pull out a bucket of shoe-shining tools and spend the evening meticulously shining his boots for the next morning. I remember the smell of the polish every time I think of it and the sound of the soft bristles of his brush swishing across the toes of his boots. Dad loved the small details on Sunday mornings when he'd dress up. He even went so far as to have his initials embroidered in cursive on the cuff of all his Sunday dress-shirt sleeves. And even now that is still one of the most endearing things I love about my daddy . . . when he dresses up and puts his best foot forward. His effort makes me smile and appreciate how he takes pride in himself, his bride, and his family. I *love* that. However, that is why I can *never* understand why he wouldn't just put a dang lid on his drinks to preserve the effort he spent on his dressed-to-the-nines details.

As he made his way to the icy cold car, it felt as though it was in slow-motion. The man took three steps down icy porch steps, and I felt all our breath let out when he made it to the ground safely. We were all waiting for the inevitable fall. As dapper a dresser as Dad is, he is equally a klutz. And this moment was a sure setup. He took several more steps, and we were rather impressed. You'd think we were watching a Cirque du Soleil show in its jaw-dropping finale scene. We practically let out an *oooh* and *ahhh* with

Simple joys are found in our retelling.

each step. To the delight of his audience, he reached out to grab the handle of the car door with the hand that was holding the Bible. With just a thumb and finger and a pretty loud grunt, he pulled ajar the nearly twenty-pound metal door and made sure it was locked into position so it wouldn't close on him. Whew! He did it! We were all in disbelief. Hooray for Larry!

Once we all took a sigh of relief and shifted to face forward, we saw Dad take a plunge backward. It looked as if he were performing a trust fall, but there was no friend standing behind him. As he fell, the coffee in his uncovered cup danced up toward the heavens before its descent. Not only did Dad slip and fall on that driveway, but he

THE COFFEE IN HIS UNCOVERED CUP DANCED UP TOWARD THE HEAVENS BEFORE ITS DESCENT.

became slightly wedged under the car, aided by gravity and ice. I wish I could say we were a family that rushed to help when someone fell like that (and if we thought for a second that he were seriously injured we would have). But not this time. We lost it after Mom revealed a sly side-smile and yelled out, "Well . . . LARRY! What in the world?!" I don't even remember if we made it to church that morning or not. I only know that we laughed and laughed. And laughed and laughed some more.

———

Every time my family gets together as grown children with our parents and our individual families, we relive these stories. For me, this story of my dad and his peculiar coffee habit is one of my personal favorites. My brothers and sisters tell me I miss pieces of the story, or I forget certain aspects here and there or substitute one moment for another. We talk over and interrupt each other, course-correcting the conversation and laughing all the while in the retelling. And if you're someone who has never been at a meal or dinner table with us, this is what you get: You get all the stories. All the favorite memories of when we laughed and lived it up. Every Thanksgiving or Christmas Day we sit for hours and reminisce. Sometimes that is all we do. No matter the new board game or fun trivia questions we aim to play that year, we end up telling stories like these. Do you know the feeling I get every time we begin to share the stories we have all heard over and over again? You guessed

THE MOST UNDERRATED TOOL WE HAVE AT OUR DISPOSAL TO SHIFT AN ATMOSPHERE OF ANXIETY TO ONE OF JOY IS TO SPEAK OUT THE GOOD TIMES.

it: joy. There's something beautiful in recalling good days with the people who love you and who know you deeper than any others on this planet.

Recently I asked a few friends to share a story or two of their favorite memories with me that fill them with joy every time they come to mind. I did this to jog my memory while writing this book about uncovering simple joys . . . but as friends flooded in my inbox, texts, and messenger app, I found myself smiling. I felt an instant connection to whomever had sent me their memory. And I would think of ways I could clear my schedule and make time to see that person again—to find them in a coffee shop or share a basket of chips and queso.

The most underrated tool we have at our disposal to shift an atmosphere of anxiety to one of joy is to speak out the good times. Why do you think life has both good and not-so-good days? The good days fill us up with a reserve of strength to sustain us when we're visited by the other days. When I am in the emotional pits, I rely on my memories of the good days to push me through, change my focus, and shift my thoughts to look for good around every corner.

I encourage you to keep a journal of some of your go-to, simple joy memories to sustain you. The retelling leads to the strength, friendships, and authenticity that always accompany genuine joy.

So go ahead. Get lost in your good stories today. That memory bank may be a deep well of much needed water to quench a joy-thirsty soul.

What is one of your favorite memories you love to retell? What is it about that particular story that continues to bring you joy?

_____

_____

_____

_____

_____

_____

_____

_____

_____

_____

SIMPLE JOYS

_____

_____

_____

_____

_____

_____

_____

_____

_____

_____

_____

_____

_____

Five

THE DAY INADEQUACY TRIED
TO SQUASH MY JOY

Mommin' is hard, y'all. This statement is not a complaint. This is not a subtle way to beg for relief troops to be sent my way. Nor is it a plea for more alone time and massage sessions with hot stones drenched in essential oils. (But I wouldn't turn that down.) This is just a well-known fact to any and every woman who has held the title of Mom.

I remember the moment I heard the proverbial

biological clock begin to tick. I knew the very day I said "I do" to Mr. Chris Payne at age twenty-two that I wanted to be the mother of his children by age thirty. For some reason, thirty always seemed old to me. *Gah.* If I could tell my younger self anything, I would correct that lie for sure. Thirty is when I really felt my life begin. I was a young wife aching for kids—the "next" stage in our marriage. I found myself overseas in Zambia, Africa, on a mission trip, crying most of the night and asking God to put my husband and me in a unified mind-set concerning the right time to start trying for a family. I got home, and we both agreed it was time.

We became pregnant fairly quickly. Within a few short weeks of that conversation, we were buying a home; registering for baby shower wishes, wants, and needs; and dreaming of a future that seemed bright with endless possibilities. I was so excited to be a momma. I was even more excited to see my guy step into the role of daddy. My pregnancy brought high risks and issues I couldn't have known or imagined in my naivety. But I soon became well acquainted with specialists, dietitians, OB-GYNs, and insulin injections. I never had to resign to bed rest, but I would find myself winded, tired, and groggy at the end of the day, refusing to leave my bed for anything other than restroom breaks. I found myself binge-watching TLC's *A Baby Story* and anything on HGTV. They were my escape from reality. Inevitably I would bawl my eyes out when watching a new mommy and daddy welcome their baby into this world for the first time. I loved it. It gave me *all* the feels. (Never mind the hormone fluctuations that aided those feels.)

My baby story was honestly a beautiful one as well. Of course, I think every momma thinks that at some level. But there was one thing that I felt was missing the moment I gave birth to both of my kiddos. In every TV episode, when the parents would first lay eyes on their child, they would cry tears of joy. So I just knew that was what I would do as well, right? Wrong. No tears. Not a single one.

Was I even human? Sheesh. Talk about needing to evaluate if I had a heart of stone. Instead, I smiled as big as I could smile and introduced myself just as I would to a new friend when asked to shake a stranger's hand at church: "Hi there! I'm your momma! I'm so glad to meet you! Do you know how long I've waited to meet you? I am going to love you all my life." (Okay, so maybe that last part is not something I'd say when meeting a complete stranger. But you get the picture: I somehow managed to be awkward when introducing myself to my children.)

Following introductions usually came a food or meal request to my nurse or husband. Typically it'd be a plea for a juicy Whataburger or fast-food taco. Mommas got to eat. Birthing is hard and hungry work.

After I met my daughter, my firstborn, I spent the next day getting acquainted with her feeding rhythms and diaper-changing needs as every new parent does. I was in love all over again. Yet this time with a little, tiny human who depended on Chris and me for every need. The day we got to take her home from the hospital, we drove about ten miles under the speed limit and were the most cautious we'd ever been behind the wheel of a car. We got home and navigated how to carry in the car seat, sat it down on the floor near our dining room table, and dared not take her out until she woke up on her own from her peaceful slumber.

Chris and I shared a meal and looked at each other in disbelief of our new reality. We had another person sharing our home with us. A new person after living nearly seven years alone with just ourselves. Not only that, we were both curious as to why they allowed us to leave the hospital with her. I mean,

I HAD NEVER FELT MORE TERRIFIED THAN I WAS IN THAT MOMENT. AND YET I HAD NEVER FELT MORE DETERMINED.

we didn't have a license or take a test to show we were qualified for the task at hand. They merely discharged us, walked us outside, and sent us home. I had never felt more terrified than I was in that moment. And yet I had never felt more determined. I was sure I was going to be a good mom and Chris was going to be a good dad.

In a matter of days, though, was when the mommin' got really difficult. After a series of depressing and harmful thoughts, I began to realize I was experiencing more than just my hormones and blood sugar levels regulating back to normal. I knew I was experiencing postpartum depression. The thoughts I would think about my husband were frightening. And even more disturbing were the thoughts I harbored in isolation. I felt disqualified before I even tried. I felt as though I would ruin another's life, and I couldn't handle the thought of who I would become if that sentiment were indeed true.

Just when I began to gain clarity and come out

on the other side of this dark depression, I became pregnant with my son. I know. We really did try to prevent that from happening. As a matter of fact, we were on three forms of birth control. So you cannot tell me that my son is not a miracle child. We certainly wanted another child; we just didn't count on it so soon after having the first one. Nevertheless, within fourteen months of welcoming our daughter into our home, we welcomed our son.

Our daughter, Cadence, was always just a smidge behind average developmental mile markers, especially when it came to her motor skills. The day I brought my son home from the hospital, Cadence was still not walking unassisted. She'd grasp at the furniture to steady herself as she made her way around a room. But she hesitated at letting go and walking unassisted until she saw her little brother. Now imagine what Chris and I were feeling. We officially went from just being open to the concept of having a family to having that family become a full-blown reality within two years. And let's not forget that meant I was pregnant for nearly two years of my life and our marriage. Yikes. It was a breeding ground for sarcasm and quick whips, but all the while it was wonderful as we embraced these two miracles in our hearts and home. For that time, though, we had both a baby who couldn't talk and a baby who couldn't walk depending on us for everything.

I remember the first day I was alone with both of my children. Any new momma knows this day. It's when all the relatives who have come to help with the new baby have left *and* the husband has to go back to work. I gotta be real. I didn't think I was going to make it. That day I had to take Duncan, my then two-week-old son, to a much-needed checkup to make sure he was eating enough, gaining weight, and remaining

I DID WHAT ANY NEW AND GOOD MOMMA WOULD DO: OVERPACK.

jaundice-free. I began to pack up the car for the first trip out being the only responsible adult. Frightening. So I did what any new and good momma would do: overpack. I hurriedly grabbed an ungodly amount of diapers in each of their appropriate sizes, a full pack of unopened wet wipes for each child, three outfit changes each, formula, bottles, juice cups, goldfish crackers, Cheerios, rattles, chew toys, stuffed animals, plastic chain-link toys, and, well, everything except the kitchen sink. I managed to fit all of this in two divided diaper bags that were roughly the size of a large carry-on piece of luggage. I slung one over each shoulder to hang diagonally across my body, picked up Cadence and held her against my hip, and did a bicep curl to lift the infant car seat carrier holding Duncan.

We made our way to the checkup with a manageable amount of gurgles and fusses. We pulled into the parking spot, and I successfully carried all the things into the office, all while managing to open my own doors and push buttons in elevators to get us where we needed to go. I was feeling pretty boss by this point. I mean, this was going remarkably well. That is, until I needed to undress Duncan to have his weight checked and change his diaper.

Listen. There needs to be a course for how to change boy diapers versus girl diapers. I had no clue that any hint of cool air making its way in the diaper area of a boy could cause him to lose all control and pee again. And little did I know the trajectory a boy could achieve if he got wind in just the wrong place at just the right time. Three onesies later and I realized I was not getting the hang of this. I had one chance—outfit—left. I felt rushed because my daughter was nearing her toddler naptime. And all the mommas know that you don't screw with nap routines. It could very well destroy every subsequent activity thereafter. Also I knew they needed this room for the next patient. We needed to get out as soon as possible. But there was no "ASAP" happening in that room

other than the cold rush of air hitting my son and him shooting himself and his clean clothes until soaked. It was awful. I took out the last baby outfit, while I stood fully drenched myself, and prayed like never before that he'd not pee on himself or me. I removed his diaper and watched as a perfect fountain-styled stream shot all the way in the air, only to land and puddle in his own ear. To this day I don't even know how it was possible. The kid was talented, I'll give him that. But at this point we were without any clean clothes. Instead, I took the paper from the exam table, wrapped him like a baby burrito, and laid him in the car seat. I tore holes where the buckles would need to go and covered him with the only remaining dry cloth I had: a baby blanket. Then I rushed to load up everything in the same order once again, making sure nothing and no one was left behind before struggling to the car to try to make it home in one piece.

I got home all right, not feeling nearly as fierce and bad mamma jamma as I did before I left the house. But I made it. I took my daughter to her room and laid her down for her afternoon nap, and I left my son in his infant seat—which also fit in a free-standing baby swing—in order to keep him asleep. Every now and then he would rustle in the makeshift paper outfit I'd made for him. But overall he stayed asleep for the next thirty minutes.

In those thirty minutes I felt so inadequate.

I cried.

I made myself a cup of coffee.

And then I cried some more.

In that moment I realized that feelings of inadequacy could either overwhelm me or spur me on to be a better momma.

I REALIZED THAT FEELINGS OF INADEQUACY COULD EITHER OVERWHELM ME OR SPUR ME ON TO BE A BETTER MOMMA.

———

When I retell this story today, I laugh to think how much I wanted to know everything and have everything together. Looking back, I didn't do so bad. I mean, no one was emotionally scarred or actually suffered harm. But in that very real time of feeling as if I was doing a job I didn't feel qualified for or equipped to do, I didn't feel that much joy at all. And yet when I look back, I smile.

Sometimes you cannot see the simple joys amidst the chaos of trying to keep everything together. But that wasn't the worst day, or nearly the hardest, in this life of being a momma. Sometimes your simple joy may not be so evident until the chaos clears.

I hope that offers you a silver lining for any discouragement you might be experiencing.

The best way I know to fight feelings of inadequacy during chaotic change in my life is to know that there will come a day I can look back and laugh.

I get it. Some days you need the cup of coffee and the ugly cry more than a good chuckle. But as every momma knows, the sum of all the days (whether chaotic, inadequate, off schedule, planned, unplanned, tired, fun, imperfect, or perfect) leads to simple joys that will forever be cherished not only in the memories but in the heart as well.

Hold on, friend. Simple joys may be hard to feel today, but they will flood your heart and mind one day down the road.

Hopefully sooner rather than later.

What makes you feel inadequate? Are there any simple joys you can focus on when those emotions invade your heart and mind?

_____

_____

_____

_____

_____

_____

_____

_____

_____

_____

SIMPLE JOYS

_____

_____

_____

_____

_____

_____

_____

_____

_____

_____

_____

_____

_____

THE LORD IS GOOD, A Refuge IN TIMES OF TROUBLE. HE CARES FOR THOSE WHO TRUST IN HIM.

NAHUM 1:7

RUN FOR COVER

For a short season I was on staff at a church doing three part-time jobs wrapped in one. The first job was coordinating the drama team and leaders needed to put on a church service designed for children in kindergarten through fifth grade. My second job was creating graphic design and communication materials for the church. And last, I was leading a worship band and coordinating the music for the young adult service that met on Wednesday evenings. Have you ever heard the saying that 20 percent of active church members do 80 percent of the work? Well, count me in that 20 percent during that season. But I loved it! I loved the hustle and bustle and responsibility. I cherished working with people I loved and admired and the lessons I was learning from the responsibility I had. Not only that, I was not yet a mom, so I had the ambition and time of a woman without children.

I had made the job my everything. I felt purpose in it, and I thought I was doing well. I got to use my creative abilities and gifts in each and every aspect. I also got to spend time developing deep relationships. I was expected to know and love on the people

I LEARNED SO MANY THINGS IN THAT SEASON. IT WAS WHAT EVERYONE DREAMS OF: A JOB WHERE YOU CAN USE ALL YOUR TALENTS, GIFTS, ABILITIES, AND PASSIONS.

I was serving and leading in worship. And I had the freedom to express my own personality in the way I approached and designed communications. I learned so many things in that season. It was what everyone dreams of: a job in which you can use all your talents, gifts, abilities, and passions.

The people I worked with were not just coworkers; they were people I grew deep friendships with and who shared many moments of highs and lows. Memories I have from those years are still some of my favorite simple joys ever.

I recall one Wednesday evening in particular. It was springtime in Texas. Now, that phrase may not mean much to you. But for anyone who lives in Texas, you know exactly what that means. The weather is unpredictable and can be pretty scary. I know—spring is supposed to be all flowers and new life blossoming and bright, sunshining days. Well, give it a couple hours and the atmosphere can change to a thunderous lightning and hail storm faster than you can flip a pancake. I have witnessed hail the size of softballs drop from the sky within thirty minutes of what seemed like a beautiful, uninterrupted spring day with my kids at the local playground. I don't know why God made Texas as weather-sporadic as He did. I have just learned how to cope when it happens. This particular Wednesday we were watching the weather reports warning of a torrential downpour and heaving thunderstorms in our area. As leaders for a midweek service, we had to make the decision to let the young adults get rides to the church (or even scarier, drive themselves as newly licensed teen drivers), wait out the storm as we proceeded with our service, or cancel it altogether. Well, in the hours preceding such a decision, we lost power to our church building as the storm increased in intensity. So that made for an easy decision. We would keep everyone safe and sound and in their own homes and try again the next Wednesday evening.

With the freed-up evening and not many places

still with power, my husband and I invited our leadership team over to our home for dinner. Not to brag, but I was making a Crock-Pot full of my famous chili. Some of you may be under the assumption that chili is a fall dish. Well, honey, I say chili is a staple in my home no matter the season. I had plenty of corn chips, shredded sharp cheddar cheese, and chopped-up purple onion to share. And most importantly, the electricity was still working at our place. So we welcomed two other married couples (Joel and Heather, and Craig and Kristi) and our one single friend who was our age (Jeff) over to our house. We *love* Jeff. He is hilarious and stands a head above (quite literally) the crowd. He is tall and burly. And loud. If you thought I was loud, you have not met Jeff. He has the ability to own a room when he walks in, mainly because his greeting is loud enough to make everyone pause, turn their head toward the door, and ask, "What was that?" No worries, people. It's just Jeff. Jeff has a way of keeping us in stitches.

He always has a joke and never has a filter for most anything he says. Jeff is "my people."

As everyone filled a bowl with my yummy chili and stayed dry and fed, we began to gather around the dinner table in my dining room. Now, I have to describe this scene for you in order to truly portray what happened that evening and what makes it so remarkable it gets its own chapter. My dining room was built in the 1980s. It's not that big at all. As a matter of fact, it can barely hold a table and chairs. When you are a guest, you have to get everything you need or want before you sit down because if you're going to get up for any reason whatsoever, you're gonna have to shimmy. It's that small of a space. We have an old round table and chairs that can comfortably seat six adults. I have tested how many it can uncomfortably seat, and it is actually many more. Don't judge. We love having people over; we just don't necessarily have the space. All that to say we had seven adults that evening in our house enjoying some delicious chili Frito pie. I love the energy of having a full house over for a meal. Especially when people feel at home enough to make their own plate, rummage the fridge for their own drink, and really sit back as though it is their home too. I think this is a lesson I learned from my momma's example growing up. No matter where we were living, big or small, my mom had a way of making any house feel like a home. So you better know that if you're invited over to my place, there is no fancy china or four-course nothin'. Just get comfy, figure out where everything is, and make yourself at home.

WE ALL WERE GLAD TO ENJOY A WARM MEAL ON AN UNEXPECTED NIGHT AWAY FROM PREVIOUSLY PLANNED RESPONSIBILITIES.

The rain was pattering harder and harder on the windows as we filled the air with laughter, stories, and watercooler conversations. We all were glad to enjoy a warm meal on an unexpected night away from previously planned responsibilities. It was as if we had reversed roles with the teenagers we were responsible for at church and were playing hooky from school. As our guests took a seat in the dining room, we realized quickly we needed an extra seat for Jeff. Now, Jeff's head wasn't that far away from our modest eight-foot ceiling, but he insisted he would rather stand. (I think it's because he didn't want to shimmy out when he wanted seconds on that awesome chili.) Lucky for Jeff, I am more insistent than he is. I brought him a chair and placed it closest to the kitchen so that he would require no shimmy whatsoever. He relented, and we all sat down to a fun meal in my humble dining room.

I truly don't remember the details of what we were talking about at the table that night. I just remember the laughing and eating and warmth I felt sitting among friends who felt like family. Then something truly memorable happened while I was talking.

I am typically not one to push my chair back from the safety of all four legs on the ground to the feeling of freedom and chance that two legs offer. It's not for me. I get my thrills elsewhere. So you know the chair I was sitting in was secure and fully on the ground as I tell you what happened next. I found myself midsentence, floundering in slow motion to grab the table. I was holding on to my chili spoon, and anything else I could try to grab, to save me from a swift and sudden descent toward the hard, ceramic tile beneath me. I don't know what or how it happened exactly, but in an instant I was topsy-turvy in a fight with gravity. All four spindle legs of that wooden chair gave way. Before I knew it, I was fully backward and flat on the ground with that entire group of friends shaking with laughter above me. Then, without warning or cause, Craig's chair did the exact same thing. Craig came crashing to the ground, and the four legs of his chair separated like a rocket ship releasing unwanted parts in its launch into outer space. Within a couple of minutes, we had two grown people down and no explanation why. Joel began to spit out his chili in laughter. (So there was that to clean up as well.) I looked up from the ground and saw Jeff leap from his chair. Before I could ask him if he felt something was about to give way, he stated to the room: "Welp. I'm up. Logic only proves that I am next."

Let's just stop here for a second, can we? What kind of logic proves that? Were we going from oldest to youngest? Shades of brown hair color? Or was Jeff, in fact, implying that we were going heaviest to lightest in weight? I was in a tizzy of laughter at this point. And so was everyone else at that table . . . or on the ground. My husband quickly grabbed the legs of the chairs, set them in the garage, and brought back in some metal—less attractive but more practical— replacement folding chairs. We spent the next couple of hours laughing and eating. And then eating some more. Heck, I think we even brewed a pot of coffee and filled bowls with ice cream, caramel syrup, and rainbow candy sprinkles.

We were inside, warm and dry, and our bellies were full while our friendships grew. All the while a storm outside was whistling with winds of sixty to seventy miles per hour, taking down fence panels and lightly flash-flooding our streets. But we didn't care. We were having a midweek, weekend kind of night. And we loved every second of it.

So what's the lesson here that's so intrinsic to discovering simple joys and authentic happiness? When I think of this night specifically, I find a few points that have sustained my joy in whatever season I am in.

First of all, we were facing a storm in the springtime. How many times does a figurative storm arise unexpectedly during an otherwise pleasant season in your life? You know, the days when you feel as if you've found your groove, conquered the darker days, and begin to see the light again. In times like this I've naively thought that meant I would not experience a

THE STORM may BE outside, BUT IT DOESN'T HAVE TO BE INSIDE OF you.

difficult moment in the middle of prosperity, or what I like to call "harvest seasons." But just because you may have cleared a winter season in your personal life—that last round of chemo, the first year survived as a widow or widower, knowing you've survived being an empty nester, the first moment you feel like yourself again after a brutal divorce or custody battle, or whatever your winter might have been—that doesn't mean you won't experience the occasional spring thunderstorm. Life is full of ups and downs and disappointments. It's full of financial stresses and unplanned interruptions. Yet I've heard my pastor say this year after year, and it is just beginning to make more sense to me: the storm may be outside, but it doesn't have to be inside of you.

That night back in my church-working days, my husband and I had a safe place with friends that was a shelter from whatever was happening outside. We were beginning to understand this tiny concept in full: you can find simple joys in unexpected interruptions that often look like distractions. Instead of complaining that we had to cancel everything, leaving each other to fend for ourselves, or worrying in a closet while listening to news weather reports every three minutes, we treated it as an adventure, came together, shared what we had, and laughed the night away until the storm passed.

That night allowed me to realize that simple joys can come in the midst of the fiercest storms. All you have to do is embrace the adventure in the unexpected.

YOU CAN FIND SIMPLE JOYS IN UNEXPECTED INTERRUPTIONS THAT OFTEN LOOK LIKE DISTRACTIONS.

Invite others in when you feel afraid of the storm.

Share what you have with those who need it, because you realize you're not the only one affected by the storm.

And find joy in the company of those in the shelter with you.

If you could have an unexpected night away from previously planned responsibilities, what would you want to be doing and who would you want to be spending that time with?

_____

_____

_____

_____

_____

_____

_____

_____

_____

_____

_____

_____

_____

_____

_____

_____

_____

_____

_____

_____

_____

_____

_____

_____

_____

CALL TO ME and I will ANSWER YOU and tell you GREAT and UNSEARCHABLE THINGS you do not know.

JEREMIAH 33:3

Seven

SELFIES WITH THE LAST WHITE RHINOS IN ZAMBIA

Have you ever wanted to help out and do good, but it didn't quite turn out as you imagined it would? Instead, everything you did to try to help actually made things much worse? I went on a missionary trip to Zambia in Africa to help students in an orphanage and adults in the community, and it felt exactly like that.

To prepare for this mission trip we had meetings

and planned for nearly ten months in advance. We dreamed up fun, recreational games to teach the children. We packed suitcases of toys and supplies for the kids to make it the most memorable and fun experience we could think of. I was incredibly excited because I had never been overseas. On top of planning a fun, summer-camp-style curriculum with our team, I was busy getting all the travel documents and vaccinations I needed to make the trip.

Every time I went to the store to do my daily errands in the months before we would leave, I inevitably thought of something else I might want to take with me to give away or use. I honestly felt as if a year of my life was spent just hoping for what I couldn't see. And everything I did was part of the effort of that unknown journey. I was pumped! The day finally came to leave, and I had packed my luggage according to the rules given by the airline for international travel to that area of the world. I also had an additional piece of luggage that would hold only things we needed to take to make the summer camp fun. We found it was much more cost-effective to do this instead of trying to ship things separately beforehand. Before we knew it, we were boarding a plane with passports in hand for our twelve-hour flight. It was crazy. I'd never flown that many consecutive hours before. Until that trip I didn't even know it was possible for a plane to stay in the air that long. After a small layover in London, we arrived in Zambia.

INSTEAD OF A CONCRETE JUNGLE, WE SAW PLAINS OF GRASS AND WIDE-OPEN SPACES WITH ANIMALS. AND THE SUNSETS SEEMED TO HAVE NO END. IT ALL WAS MAGICAL. I WAS IN AWE.

The Zambian sky was a bright blue, and the weather was a perfect seventy-three degrees with not a rain cloud in sight. The earth felt untouched by modern technology and conveniences. As a matter of fact, it felt as though I had traveled back to a much simpler time. Instead of a concrete jungle, we saw plains of grass and wide-open spaces with animals. And the sunsets seemed to have no end. It all was magical. I was in awe.

Now, I guess I didn't pay enough attention during our planning meetings, because I thought we'd get off the plane we'd been on for nearly a day and go straight to our rooms to freshen up and grab a quick shower. Well, that's not what happened. Instead, we met our contact at the airport, and he ushered us and our luggage onto a vehicle that was kind of like a short bus. Rather than going straight to where we were staying and taking a load off, we found our-selves on a five-hour bus ride to reach our location.

We did, however, stop at a little roadside café in

the middle of nowhere to find something to silence the hungry growls of our tummies. I looked at the menu and was quickly reminded I was not in America anymore. I found what looked to be the most American thing I could find and ordered it. We are so used to food coming to our tables quickly in America. What I didn't realize until then was that they cooked everything from scratch when ordered . . . in much less sophisticated kitchens and with no electricity. So I sat, waiting a hot minute for my Zambian hamburger with cheese and french fries. When it finally came to the table, it looked yummy. The sweet lady also brought red and yellow condiment squeeze jars. Typically in America the red one will be filled with ketchup and the yellow with mustard. So I opened the bun of my cheeseburger and squirted the ketchup first. Oh man. It looked so tasty. Delicious, even. I couldn't wait to bite in. But why not go for the good stuff? YOLO! I ended up grabbing what I assumed was mustard and squeezed it hard over my burger.

Y'all. Apparently they don't do mustard in yellow bottles. Nope. They like a different condiment for their fries: vinegar. So I was shooting straight-up vinegar all over my burger, and it even soaked through the bun. At this point I thought, *Well, it's an adventure, right?* Plus, I knew how long it took to make and didn't dare ask for another.

Upon finishing our meal, we all took turns taking a restroom break before boarding the bus one more time for the last leg of the trip. I was the last of the team to go. I came out of the restroom to see everyone had already boarded the bus, and it was already running, prepared for departure. I sauntered slowly toward it, and *it left* mid-saunter. No joke—it whisked away without me on it! I typically don't run, but if ever I had a reason to do so, it was right then and there. I stopped running and waving my arms back and forth about half a mile down the dirt road once I saw the bus's brake lights come on. And then the reverse lights. To this day, this is why my church uses the "buddy system" while traveling. Make sure you have a buddy whenever you get off a vehicle in the middle of nowhere in a foreign country.

I got on the bus, we made our way to our lodgings, and I began to unpack some clothes from my rummaged suitcase.

Why was it rummaged, you ask? Apparently Zambian authorities working for customs at the airport had singled out and checked my luggage because it looked suspicious. *I mean.* What's suspicious about two giant Halloween-sized bags of candy, peanut butter crackers, fruit snacks, and enough beef jerky to last at least three grown men a month? To my surprise, nothing. Nothing was odd about that at all. I thought for sure they'd be judging the snack count in the suitcase I brought. But that wasn't what it was at all. Now, for a frame of reference, I was about three hundred and twenty pounds. Naturally my clothes were a bit larger and took up more space in my suitcase. So I was interrogated by Zambian custom officials who suspected I was bringing an ungodly amount of clothes to sell. I had to pull out pieces of clothing one by one and show them that there wasn't more than two weeks' worth. It was only an optical illusion because of the sheer size and volume of fabric needed to accommodate my larger frame. Cue complete embarrassment, y'all.

By the time I had straightened out my things and set up a mosquito tent to envelop the bed I'd be sleeping in for the next ten nights, I began to wonder if I had made a mistake by coming on this trip. It didn't seem I was going to be of any help at all. As a matter of fact, it felt as though I was slowing down our team. Heck, they may have subconsciously felt that way as well. I mean, they *did* leave me on the side of a remote road in the middle of Africa. I had the right heart to want to help, but nothing seemed to be going my way.

I decided to sleep off the feelings of inadequacy and try again the next day. This, I comforted myself, would be the perfect day, because we were going to

NO MISADVENTURES FROM THE PREVIOUS DAY WOULD STOP THE JOY OOZING FROM MY ANTICIPATION OF MEETING WHAT WERE SURE TO BE MY NEW BESTIES.

meet the people we had been preparing to meet the whole year. I envisioned what they might look like and how their accent might sound. I couldn't handle it. No misadventures from the previous day would stop the joy oozing from my anticipation of meeting what were sure to be my new besties. We drove a short five minutes to arrive at an orphanage where I could hear the singing and clapping of the children from outside its entrance gate. My heart started to well up with even more joy. Oh, the sound of their singing is still one of the most vivid memories of my life, and it affects me viscerally when I recall it. There's nothing quite like the pure joy in the songs they sang. The energy of each note was electric! And as we drew closer down the driveway, I locked eyes with several children rushing to greet the bus of Americans. I was one of the last ones to step off the bus, and when I did, I wanted to greet people and shake their hands—which is a custom they are used to as well, so it wouldn't have been weird. Yet every young child I offered my hand to would seem terrified and run away. What in the world was happening?! Now I was repelling the people I came to meet and love on?

One Zambian gravitated toward me, however. She was a robust and loud woman. Larger in stature, like myself. The children called her Momma Vivian. She came over and hugged everyone on our team. And when she came to me, she hugged me, pulled away with her hands still wrapped around my arm, and said these words:

"Oooooohhhh, you are fat. Very, very fat."

Now, Momma Vivian said this in a tone that I

knew to be pure joy and complimentary. She even squeezed the fattest part on the back of my arms and made her way up to another squeeze of the cheeks on my face, like you would do to an irresistible infant. To say I was confused is an understatement; yet she seemed unaffected by this declaration and went about her introductions and then led us to where we needed to unload our things.

From that moment forward, Momma Vivian and I were side by side. I don't know if I was drawn to her because she was so honest (#mypeople) or because I was slightly frightened of her. Either way, I was always by her side.

A full day went by, and I didn't feel a connection with any one child, or even the group of children as a whole, if I am being honest. Furthermore, I was given the worst compliment I have ever received when meeting someone face-to-face for the first time. My enthusiasm for staying on this trip was dwindling at a rapid pace.

The next morning Momma Vivian could tell something was wrong. She asked why I looked so sad. I told her that I wasn't connecting with the children and that they would run from me but not the others on our team. I also was vulnerable enough to ask for more clarification as to why she said what she did the day before. She told me that most women in their culture measured how healthy they were by how large they were. If you are a larger woman in Zambia, you are probably afforded luxuries that other women struggle to know every day. Things like full bellies and food for not only your children but yourself as well. It was a compliment in the highest regard. I knew that she saw me as a healthy and wealthy woman in her culture—not something I would ever be labeled in America. So that was an easy misunderstanding and explanation. I turned from feelings of shame to feelings of honor in an instant. But the explanation about why the children would run from me is one that I never could have seen coming.

Momma Vivian began to tell me that it had to do with a bit of folklore that region of Zambia passed along and adopted. Do you know the story of the boogie man in American folklore? From my understanding, it was a way (admittedly not the best way) to inspire discipline and obedience in your children. Yes, ages ago we would invoke fear in our kids if they misbehaved. Parents would tell their kids that if they didn't follow the rules a boogie man would come and snatch them up at night. I am not condoning this at all. I want to be very clear. I am just setting out for you the origins of this tale so you can further grasp what Momma V began to tell me next. She informed me that they have a similar tradition in their culture. But instead of a boogie man, they tell their children that a large, fat white woman is going to come eat them if they misbehave! What the mess? Are you kidding me? No wonder children were frightened of me every time I offered my hand for a handshake! I looked as if I had already snacked on two toddlers prior to meeting them that day!

Let's just say that I spent more time hanging with the local women than I did with the children. But I actually loved that. I got to see how they talked with each other, gossiped, made their meals, and served their families. I was able to ask intimate questions I'd never ask them in a public setting. So it didn't turn out the way I had planned for nearly a year before, but it turned out even better. I was invited into a sacred space where very few are allowed. And I got to see women do what they do best: shine and radiate pure joy!

When it was time to say good-bye to Momma Vivian, we both cried. I hugged her like a long-lost sister and genuinely didn't want to leave. But I knew we needed to start our trek back to the airport. We had several hours to drive and wanted to make sure we were rested before we began the long flight home. I did get to see her again on a trip the next year. Yes,

I decided to go back again. Call me crazy or in love with adventure, but Africa, despite all her efforts to derail me, had made me fall in love with her.

On that first trip we decided to detour on our way back to the airport and get some much-needed rest before boarding our plane. We discovered that one of the Seven Wonders of the World, Victoria Falls, was nearly on our way. We went to the falls for a few hours, and we all purchased ponchos because it was the rainy season. All the extra water made the spray from the falls so furiously strong you'd get drenched just walking several feet away from it.

I walked slowly toward a lookout point that opened up to reveal a view of the falls. I began hearing the roar of the falls over everything else, even before I saw them. If they were half as beautiful as they were loud, I knew I would be impressed. And I certainly discovered why Victoria Falls is a wonder of our world. There are no descriptive words that I could muster up to describe their beauty. Even if you google images of Victoria Falls, which I highly suggest you do when you finish this chapter, it is nothing like being there and hearing the roar of the water as it makes its dangerous tumble toward the ground. The more I familiarized myself with the sound and sheer beauty of what I was seeing, the braver and less cautious I became. I began to run from viewpoint to viewpoint—landing to landing—to take in all the views and all the wonder. I found myself laughing the whole time. I couldn't help it. It was a reaction I've never before had to the beauty of nature. I felt joy in every majestic moment of this discovery.

We gathered around the bus at the designated time we had agreed to leave. (I was a few minutes early. I learned my lesson, y'all. I was not about to be left a second time.) Then we drove on toward a place that would have a warm bed for us that night before we started the long flight home the next morning. We were staying at a game reserve. When we arrived we were led on a small driving tour in search of African animals native to that area. This was way beyond a zoo. It was utterly amazing. We quietly stalked the grasslands and came upon the likes of antelope, wildebeests, zebras, and several giraffes. Our guide from the reserve asked if we wanted to see something extra special. *Of course* we did! He grabbed his rifle, made his way off the bus, and asked us to follow him quietly off the beaten path. Although this was going against every instinct I had in me, I was still on a bit of a reckless high from the playtime we'd just experienced at Victoria Falls. So, like everyone else, I jumped off the bus to see what might lie hidden in the landscape.

The guide informed us that we were heading to see the only remaining male and female white rhinos in all of Zambia. It was the hottest part of the day for them, and they would typically rest under a certain shade tree, where he was leading us. As I neared our guide, I whispered to him, "Is that gun you're carrying to protect us from an animal if it attacks us?"

SIMPLE joys ARE ALWAYS FOUND IN BOTH adventure AND misadventure.

He looked at me as though I had asked him something that was so far-fetched he didn't even know how to respond. He quickly told me that his gun was not to protect me but to protect the animals. It was then I realized I may need to run one more time on this Zambian adventure. I positioned myself at the end of the line to see the rhinos, thinking that if we were charged, I could get a head start in running away before everyone else.

At last we reached the shade tree leaning over the most beautiful creatures I'd ever seen that close up. Sure, there was no fence protecting me, but safety wasn't my main concern in that moment. I saw a peaceful nap between two love-struck rhinos. We were informed that the momma was, indeed, pregnant (a miracle in the face of poaching and the threat of extinction at that time). I grabbed my disposable camera (because, well, these were actually the bee's knees back then) and took a selfie (before selfies were cool) with the proud mom and dad. And, to my surprise, I was struck with such awe and profound wonder at where I was standing and what I was experiencing that my eyes flooded with tears the moment I put the camera in my backpack. It all overwhelmed me at one time. The sum of every day of that short-term mission trip hit me with all the feels as I looked at where I was standing.

Some moments of joy are a struggle to find in the days that seem to go all sorts of wrong. Yet they're there. It would have been really easy to give up mentally on Africa within the first few days of the mission trip, and even upon arrival during my customs debacle.

I FIND MYSELF LOOKING BACK WITH SUCH WONDER AND AWE AT THE HIDDEN MOMENTS OF JOY THAT I DISCOVERED IN THE MOST UNLIKELY OF PLACES.

But I didn't. And now I find myself looking back with such wonder and awe at the hidden moments of joy that I discovered in the most unlikely of places.

If there's anything I have learned about joy from beautiful Africa, its people, and its atmosphere, it's this: simple joys stay the course through misunderstandings, detours, and differences, and often lead to the most magical and wonder-filled experiences you could never predict.

I am so grateful that trip was nothing like I had planned.

I am grateful because I got to see what I wasn't looking for, and it was far better than what I was expecting.

———

Some of you may be struggling with the idea of finding joy in your life because your plans are unraveling. You may be misunderstood. You may even be the weakest and slowest in the group you're with and just trying to keep up. I want to encourage you. Lift up your head, go with the flow, and look around. There may be more wonder in the journey than you can currently see hiding behind your worry.

Just one final word of wisdom: If you're ever in Zambia and you could be mistaken for a large, white woman who eats misbehaving children, don't visit an orphanage, and don't admire how beautiful the children are by saying aloud, "Oh, my word! These children are so adorable, I could just *eat them up*!"

I'm just saying. It doesn't go over well.

SIMPLE JOYS

Where is the most unlikely place you've discovered joy?

_____

_____

_____

_____

_____

_____

_____

_____

_____

_____

_____

_____

_____

_____

_____

_____

_____

_____

_____

_____

_____

_____

_____

_____

TAKE THE GOOD, TOSS THE BAD

Gospel singin' was an important part of the years that would follow the night I gave my heart to Jesus. I would practice singing our own songs with my cousins and siblings. My mom even had a fun gospel group with her siblings that she sang in as well. If we were having a family reunion or a get-together, you better believe that we would have some singin' too. And at the helm of it all was my sweet grandpa and grandma, Omer and Annie Mae Suiter, singing classic hymns and heart songs.

I WANTED TO BE JUST LIKE HIM. BUT I DIDN'T HAVE A GUITAR, AND HE LIVED SO FAR AWAY THAT I WAS SURE I COULDN'T PICK UP THE SKILL.

My grandpa Suiter was the real deal. While we were all fiddling around with accompaniment tracks, he was playing guitar and harmonica at the same time. Seriously. He'd wear a brace that would hold the harmonica in place near his lips so his hands would be free to play guitar. Somehow between verses and chorus, when he needed to play a harmonic line, he'd whip his jaw to the side of the brace and pull it forward and impress us all. Well, maybe just me. But I couldn't take my eyes off how talented he was! I was more than impressed. I wanted to be just like him. But I didn't have a guitar, and he lived so far away that

I was sure I couldn't pick up the skill. Nevertheless, at the age of fourteen, I had a dream that I was playing a guitar just like my granddaddy. And in that dream, I also felt a part of my future was waiting to be explored. So I began to practice and play after being gifted a guitar that following Christmas.

Guitar playing became an instant bond between me and Grandpa Suiter. Now when we would gather together, I'd bring my own guitar and find some time to steal away and sit at his feet with folded legs on the carpet, mimicking his every strum. I was a student of his every move, and I loved it! He'd teach me the old hymns that I would beg to learn, and he'd share with me the new songs he'd been plucking around with that were still imperfect. I'd watch him light up as he captivated a most unlikely audience: his grandkids. We became closer and closer through those sweet songs. When I hear some of them today, I tear up instantly. All because I can hear the crackle in his broken voice as he sang with passion and conviction the lyrics that made him a man worthy of imitation.

For a short season following my college years, I got to live with my grandma and grandpa Suiter because they moved in with my parents. It was incredibly fun being able to pick and grin with Grandpa anytime we liked. One morning that I'll never forget, Grandpa came down the stairs with his prized, six-stringed, acoustic-electric guitar in hand. He was holding it out with tears bubbling in his eyes, and he headed toward me as I sat on the couch. He pushed it out in a firm way and said, "Here." Well, before I could ask a question, his voice began to tremble, and he made a statement through tears that I will never forget: "I was upstairs practicing some new songs, and God told me clear as day to give this to you." He pushed out the guitar a little farther, pressing it closer to my grasp.

I said, "Grandpa, you don't have to give that to me now, just save it for me later. You love that guitar. It's your favorite. Keep it. I'll take care of it when you're through with it." Grandpa leaned the guitar against the couch where I was sitting and said firmly, "Candy, when God tells you to do something, you do it right then and there. God has a plan for you and this guitar. No arguin', now. You hear?" And when Grandpa ended a statement with "you hear?" well, there really was no arguing after that. I stood up, hugged his neck, and cried a bit with him.

To this day, that is my favorite guitar. It is my most prized possession. Grandpa asks if I've been playing it nearly every time I see him, if I am not the first to confess that I have. When I think about these memories of faith and the roots I have been given in my

I BELIEVE ALL OF US HAVE AN INHERITANCE THAT COMES FROM OUR FAMILIES, WHETHER FINANCIAL OR EMOTIONAL.

family, I realize this: simple joys are often found in deep-rooted faith and the legacy families create.

I believe all of us have an inheritance that comes from our families, whether financial or emotional. Although you may not have a dime left to you by the ones you have long lost, I am sure experiences and moments from the life you've lived with them have shaped you. I am not so naive as to believe that all things are as wonderful as I described in the story I've just shared with you. You see, I have some things I would rather not repeat or emulate handed down to me from my family as well. There are certain struggles I have witnessed with addictions, habits, and hangups that I would rather avoid, breaking the cycle for the family I am raising right now.

You may have a generational inheritance of things you may be inclined to pass down or repeat in your home. But do you know that when you get a check written to you, it's only valuable if you sign your name to the back, endorse it, and cash it in? You

Simple joys are often found in deep-rooted faith and the legacy families create.

may want to cash in some of the experiences you've seen within your family, and you may not want to for others.

The moments that have both shaped and sharpened my faith were forged in memories made with those who lived out what they believed right before my eyes. I have a choice to either emulate all the behaviors I witnessed, good or bad, or simply take the best and leave the rest. No matter what life throws my way, I can choose to embrace whatever joy is offered in the lessons learned from those who are closest to me. I also know I can let go of the behaviors that would ensnare me in worry, doubt, comparison, or settling for a lesser life. The beauty in all this is the power of choice. You are never too old or too far gone to take one small moment to embrace the best in your family inheritance and toss aside the worst. You have the power to change your stars. Your generational examples don't have to dictate, determine, or destroy your joy.

If you're ever going to live a life full of simple joys and deep wells of happiness, deposit the good and toss the bad. For me, I have deposited rich faith moments and memories that sustain me when I feel like giving up. Those are the deposits I draw on in my heart and mind when I think about living daily with joy. And, to be real, I have experiences and memories that I have never cashed in and never will. I've seen cycles of behavior and cynicism growing up that I refuse to repeat just because "I was raised that way."

Simple joys are found in the histories and experiences that have both made you great and challenged you to rise above and become better. Your joy will become fuller the more you realize what to deposit and what to

MAKE WHATEVER YOU SIGN YOUR NAME TO WORTH EVERY PROVERBIAL PENNY.

toss. Make whatever you sign your name to worth every proverbial penny. In the end, you're depositing into an account that will either increase or deplete your simple joys.

What aspect of your family inheritance might it benefit you to toss? And what is golden—something you need to carry with you and remember along the path of your life's journey?

_____

_____

_____

_____

_____

_____

_____

_____

_____

_____

_____

_____

_____

_____

_____

_____

_____

_____

_____

_____

_____

_____

_____

ask seek knock

AND IT WILL BE **GIVEN** TO YOU,

AND YOU WILL **FIND**,

AND THE DOOR WILL BE **OPENED** TO YOU.

FOR *EVERYONE* **WHO** ASKS *receives*; THE ONE WHO SEEKS *finds*; AND TO THE ONE WHO KNOCKS, THE DOOR WILL BE **OPENED**.

MATTHEW 7:7-8

Epilogue

PROSPECTING FOR A HEART OF GOLD

So how'd you do at prospecting for gold nuggets of joy?

Did any simple joys especially stand out to you and remind you to dig a bit deeper?

As I uncover where simple joys are hiding or find them in plain sight, I see one commonality: joy is valuable. And that makes me wonder, what do you do with the most valuable things when you find them?

Are you the type who hides them away in a box only to be opened at fancy dinner parties to wow spectators who've never seen such valuable things before? Or do you rent a safety deposit box and take your joy from knowing somewhere, someday you'll have the ability to use them if you need them? Or maybe you're the type who finds something of value and cashes it in immediately so you can acquire more.

When you prospect for joy, you'll find that you are likely to treat it as you would treat something of value. If I could encourage you in any way before you leave these pages, it would be in this: use it or lose it.

When you find the joy you've been longing for, use it. Share it. Don't hoard it or save it for a better, brighter opportunity. Be the one who cashes in on what you find so that you can invest in ways to find more. Joy is not only yours for the taking, but it's yours to use as a resource.

Above all, friends, cherish, treasure, and share your simple joys in every moment you are given. You never know, one day they may lead to extravagant joy in a way you never thought possible.

Acknowledgments

To my incredible team at HarperCollins who sees the value in simple joys and making them available to all. Thank you!

To Jana Burson and Christopher Ferebee. Thank you for being my literary agents and believing in me from the beginning.

To Shanon Stowe and Paige Collins. Thank you for the encouragement you give me every time I talk your ear off with another crazy idea or concept. You always push my visions and dreams into reality. I cannot thank you enough for how you believe in what God is doing in my life. You honor me and inspire me to do all things God has for me and never miss a simple joy along the way.

To Apple Inc. Thank you for creating the iPad Pro and the Apple Pencil. It made the work on this book much easier.

To P.F. Chang's restaurant chain. Thank you for pan-seared dumplings, lettuce wraps, and free WiFi. They were the fuel to many a Saturday sketching and writing this book.

Above all, thank you could never be enough to my best friends and my big three in my core four: Chris Payne, Cadence Payne, and Duncan Payne. You are the ones who make space for me to practice what I preach . . . ALWAYS. I love you so much.

About the Author

Candace Payne is an author, speaker, and viral sensation whose video of trying on a Chewbacca mask became the most-viewed Facebook Live video to date (170+ million views). She shares her message of joy and laughter through media appearances and a robust speaking and appearance schedule that includes women's groups, churches, festivals, conferences, and organizations around the country.

Candace's first book, *Laugh It Up!: Embrace Freedom and Experience Defiant Joy*, and the accompanying small-group curriculum, *Defiant Joy:*

What Happens When You're Full Of It, are available now. Candace lives in Texas with her husband, two children, and ornery pugs. Connect with her online at CandacePayne.me.

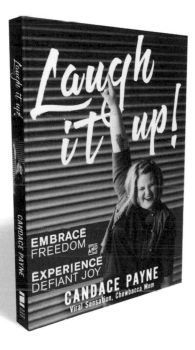

NOTES

NOTES

NOTES

NOTES

NOTES

NOTES

NOTES

_____

_____

_____

_____

_____

_____

_____

_____

_____

_____

_____

_____

_____

_____

NOTES

NOTES